ABW9457

Take a trip to

ZIMBABWE

Keith Lye

Franklin Watts

London   New York   Sydney   Toronto

Facts about Zimbabwe:

Area:
390,580 sq. km
(150,804 sq. miles)

Population:
8,667,000

Capital:
Harare

Largest cities:
Harare (656,000)
Bulawayo (414,000)
Gweru (79,000)
Mutare (70,000)

Official language:
English

Religions:
Christianity, traditional
beliefs

Main exports:
Tobacco, gold,
ferrochrome, asbestos,
cotton, nickel, sugar, iron
and steel, maize

Currency:
Zimbabwe dollar

Franklin Watts
12a Golden Square
London W1

Franklin Watts Inc.
387 Park Avenue South
New York, N.Y. 10016

ISBN: UK Edition 0 86313 535 8
ISBN: US Edition 0 531 10364 1
Library of Congress Catalog Card No:
86–51550

© Franklin Watts Limited 1987

Typeset by Ace Filmsetting Ltd
Frome, Somerset
Printed in Hong Kong

Maps: Simon Roulstone
Design: Edward Kinsey
Stamps: Stanley Gibbons Limited
Photographs: Liba Taylor 3, 4, 5, 6, 7, 8,
9, 12, 14, 15, 16, 20, 21, 22, 23, 24, 25, 26,
27, 28, 29, 30, 31; Hutchison Library 7,
12, 13, 18, 19, 22; Chris Fairclough 10
Front Cover: Liba Taylor
Back Cover: Liba Taylor

Zimbabwe is a country in southern
Africa. It was once a British colony,
called Rhodesia. It became fully
independent in 1980, when its name
was changed to Zimbabwe, after the
stone ruins at Great Zimbabwe near
Masvingo. Great Zimbabwe was built
between about AD 1000 and 1450.

The long Zambezi River forms
Zimbabwe's northern border with
Zambia. Zimbabwe is a landlocked
country, and it lies far from the sea.
European explorers did not reach it
until the 19th century.

The first European to explore the Zambezi River was the missionary David Livingstone in the 1850s. In 1855, he reached Victoria Falls. He named it after the British Queen, Victoria. His statue now stands at the Falls.

Victoria Falls is one of Africa's most spectacular sights. It is on the Zambezi River on Zimbabwe's northwestern border with Zambia. The African name for the Falls is Mosi oa Tunya, meaning "smoke that thunders."

Following the explorers, European businessmen and colonists went to southern Africa. One man, Cecil Rhodes, founded the British South Africa Company. This company occupied what is now Zimbabwe and named it Rhodesia in 1898. Rhodes died in 1902. He was buried at World's View, near Bulawayo.

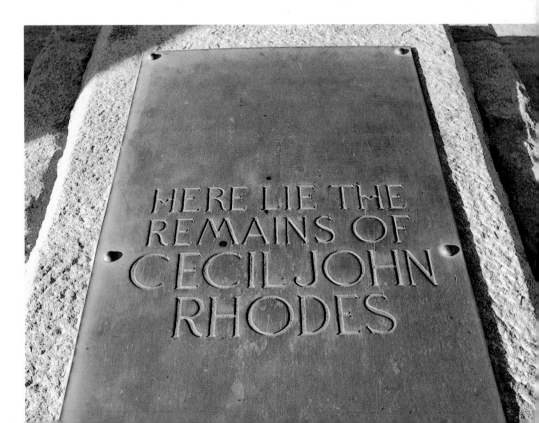

From 1898 to 1923, Rhodesia's day-to-day affairs were run by the British South Africa Company and British settlers, who arrived in large numbers. Many of them became prosperous farmers. In 1923, Rhodesia became a self-governing British colony.

The capital of Rhodesia was founded in 1890, when pioneers sent by Cecil Rhodes built a fort there. They named the fort Salisbury, after Britain's prime minister. Salisbury was renamed Harare when Zimbabwe became independent in 1980.

The picture shows some stamps used in Zimbabwe. The main unit of currency is the dollar, which is divided into 100 cents.

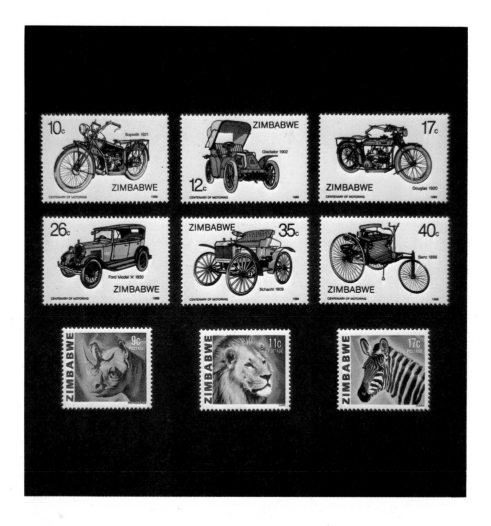

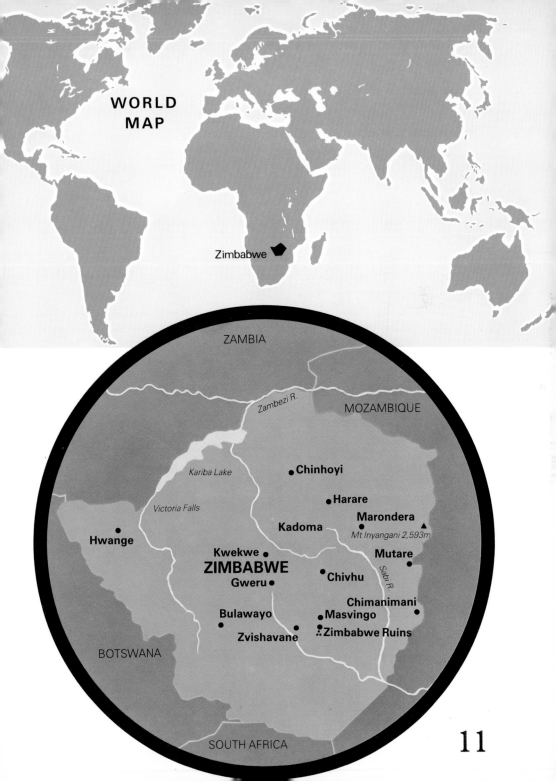

WORLD MAP

Zimbabwe

ZAMBIA

MOZAMBIQUE

Zambezi R.

Kariba Lake

●Chinhoyi

Victoria Falls

●**Harare**

Marondera

Kadoma

▲

Mt Inyangani 2,593m

●**Hwange**

Kwekwe ●

ZIMBABWE

Gweru ●

●**Chivhu**

Mutare

●

Sabi R.

Chimanimani

Bulawayo

●

●**Masvingo**

●

Zvishavane

∴**Zimbabwe Ruins**

BOTSWANA

SOUTH AFRICA

11

Zimbabwe is now a republic. Its
parliament in Harare consists of a
100-member House of Representatives
and a 40-member Senate. The
President is Head of State. The prime
minister, leader of the party with
most seats in Parliament, heads the
government.

12

Bulawayo is the second largest city after Harare. About one out of every four people lives in a city or town. The others live in villages or on farms. Zimbabwe is thinly populated. Large areas of savanna (grassland) and woodland contain few people.

Many people in Zimbabwe are
Christians, though some follow
ancient local religions. Some follow
religions which combine local beliefs
and Christianity. The picture shows
the Anglican Cathedral in Harare.

14

Most people in Zimbabwe are black Africans. About two percent are whites and one percent Asians or people of mixed descent. The main black African groups are the Shona in the north and the Ndebele in the south.

Most of Zimbabwe is a tableland, called the high veld. It lies mostly between 1,200 and 1,500 m (3,937–4,921 ft). Although Zimbabwe is in the tropics, the high veld has a pleasant climate, with about 800 mm (31 inches) of rain a year.

The highest peak, Inyangani, is situated in the east. The Eastern Highlands are wet, with an average annual rainfall of about 1,500 mm (59 inches). The driest and hottest part of Zimbabwe is a low-lying region in the south. It is called the low veld.

Zimbabwe is a poor, developing country. Farming employs 53 out of every 100 workers, as compared with 13 in industry. The chief food crop is maize (or corn). Other grains, soya beans and peanuts are also important.

Tobacco is a major export crop, as also are cotton, sugar cane and tea. The picture shows a factory in Zimbabwe where tobacco is graded and packed into bundles before it is sold at auctions in Harare.

Cattle are the most important farm animals. Many are European breeds, but humped African cattle are also common. Beef, dairy products and hides are all major farm products. Zimbabwe has about 5·5 million cattle.

Zimbabwe has several gold mines, including this one west of Harare. Other minerals produced in Zimbabwe include coal (mainly from the Hwange region), iron ore (from Kwekwe), asbestos, chrome, copper and nickel.

The Kariba Dam across the
Zambezi River was completed in
1961. Lake Kariba behind the dam
now covers about 5,200 square
km (about 2,000 square miles). A
hydroelectric power station at
Kariba supplies electricity to both
Zimbabwe and Zambia.

Many Zimbabwean factories process farm and mining products. Other manufactures include textiles, footwear, farm implements, medicines and radio equipment. The picture shows a factory near Kwekwe. Fertilizers are made in this factory.

Zimbabwe has much beautiful
scenery, historic sites and magnificent
national parks and reserves. Hwange
National Park is Zimbabwe's largest.
It contains such animals as antelopes,
buffaloes, elephants and giraffes.

24

In the 1980s, about 300,000 tourists visited Zimbabwe every year. Popular places include Victoria Falls, the Kariba Lake area, Hwange, the Eastern Highlands and Great Zimbabwe. Expert guides escort the tourists.

Living standards are rising in
Zimbabwe, especially in the cities.
This family in Harare is fortunate
enough to own a television set. There
is one television channel. In 1984, it
broadcast for 45 hours every week.

Many people in country areas are
poor. The main food is corn, which
is pounded into a flour, cooked into a
kind of porridge, and eaten hot. Many
people in Zimbabwe get less food
than they need for a healthy diet.

Primary education is now free and compulsory. In 1980, only 40 percent of children of primary school age were at school. By 1986, the percentage of children in this age range attending school had risen to 93 percent.

Many adults in Zimbabwe cannot read or write. The government has recently greatly increased the number of schools and teachers, especially in country areas. This primary school is in a farming area north of Harare.

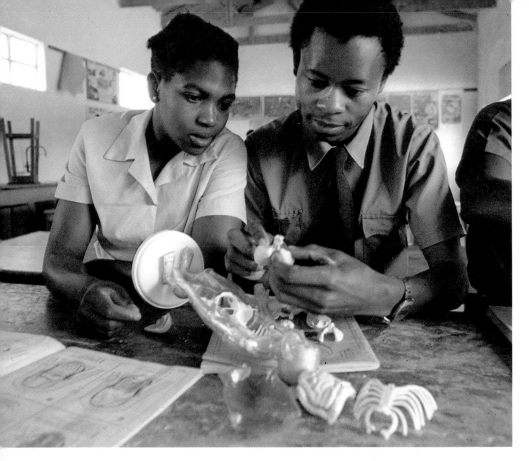

The number of secondary schools
has also increased since 1980. The
number of children at secondary
schools rose from 75,000 in 1980 to
nearly 500,000 in 1986. Parents pay
fees for the education of children at
both private and government
secondary schools.

Zimbabwe faces many problems. People live on average only 57 years, as compared with more than 70 years in developed countries. But young Zimbabweans are confident that they can help their country to develop and raise everyone's living standards.

Index